YAANOM
SARPONG OSEI ASAMOAH

This is a work of fiction. All names, characters, places, and incidents are a product of the author's imagination. Any resemblance to real events or persons, living or dead, is entirely coincidental.

Published by Akashic Books
©2024 Sarpong Osei Asamoah
ISBN: 978-1-63614-223-4

All rights reserved
Printed in China
First printing

Akashic Books
Instagram, X, Facebook: AkashicBooks
info@akashicbooks.com
www.akashicbooks.com

African Poetry Book Fund
Prairie Schooner
University of Nebraska
110 Andrews Hall
Lincoln, Nebraska 68588

*. . . only those who will risk going too far
can possibly find out just how far one can go.*
—T.S. Eliot

"How can you go too far when history already went there before you?"

* * *

For the Ancestors, Nananom Nsamanfo, Yaanom: Yaa-nom: Yaa nom: Yaa 'n'em: Yaa and folk like her: Yaa and the people with her: Yaa's people

And for Paulina Tabuah Adadey, my mother, always

TABLE OF CONTENTS

Preface by Kwame Dawes 5

Yaanom 10
Dzin 11
Testimony 12
Bless the Tide That Blesses the Boat with Wreaths 13
The End of the World Looks Like Sails 14
In the water the sun cannot hide its bruises 15
Doomsday Device 16
Yaa 17
Ahwenepa nkasa 18
Dixcove*(ry)* 19
Princes Town/Pokesu 20
At Elmina Castle I bled 21
All the saints of Elmina Castle are wet 22
Yaanom *II* 23
Requiem 24
hey Yusef Komunyakaa, *if history is human,* show me her grave 25
Mɛni aatele ni abooo? 26
Prayer is a dagger meant for God's ears 27
Magic in Inescapable Skin 28
The Tree 29
Glossary 31
Acknowledgments 32

PREFACE
by Kwame Dawes

> And in the bluest vein of that night,
> I was carrying these poems through a sunset,
> to show them what the end of the world looks like.
> ("Yaanom")

An invocation to the multilayered ancestors with whom he must contend, Ghanaian poet Sarpong Osei Asamoah's collection opens with a familiar declaration of intent—the poet invokes the song of poetry to carry out a task. In this instance, the function is prophetic and grand—the jeremiad's assurance will teeter as the collection unfolds. And it's important to note that he is not clear about the identity of "them," whether it refers to the readers of the poems or the poems themselves. In the end, the poem's strength lies in its questioning.

In "Dzin" the poet lays out the fundamental challenges of his art as a Ghanaian in the early twenty-first century. The colonial legacy lingers in the tension between his language and his mother's language, located in the reckoning he must do with the history of religion and ideas that emerge from the presence of Jesus in Ghana. What quickly grows clear is that the poet has access to archives, and from a postcolonial position, irony is his weapon. It offers a kind of respite, the irony of amazement at the audacity of British colonial exploitation:

> When I cast a spell with mother,
> my tongue returns to me, briefly, a smoke horse.
> In my mother's language I have no sugar left to make thrones out of
> without capsizing British American ships.

> In the *Jesus* name,
> the first British slave ship to arrive in Africa was *JESUS of Lübeck*,
> chartered by Queen Elizabeth I to slavers in 1562;
> they came—literally—in the name of *Jesus!*

The language he uses, namely English, has been reshaped and redirected by his mother's tongue. Confronted by that language, the poet has no capacity to praise the colonial force. This is the use of the mother's tongue: to curse or, at the very least, be an iconoclastic force against the colonizer's tongue.

Asamoah positions himself within the African Diaspora; he is both fascinated and challenged by the history of colonialism, enslavement, and the transportation of Africans from Guinea to Virginia. In "Bless the Tide that Blesses the Boat with Wreaths" (a pointed allusion to Lucille Clifton's *Blessing the Boats,*) one imagines this lamentation spoken on the coast of Virginia, a kind of monument to the Middle Passage. The poem ends with an unequivocal indictment of whiteness and white-centered Christianity. The Jesus who arrived in West Africa on the "Lübeck" will continue to betray as he is embodied by the minds and hearts of white people:

> Bless *The Boy Who Spat in Sargrenti's Eye*
> Bless the fishes who waited for us to drown
> before eating through our eyeballs
>
> Bless the white woman at the landing beach
> of the British colony of Virginia, who said,
> *Here's some water, but you can't have any,*
> *till our God falls in love with your dark skin*
> *and blesses the halo around your neck*

Asamoah invokes an invented history, rooted in the well-researched history of nineteenth-century West Africa and the historical novel *The Boy Who Spat in Sargerenti's Eye*. Gradually, we see that Asamoah's relationship to history is quite pragmatic and aggressively specific. He is drawn to lamentation, but above all, there is a way in which the instruments of history—the tools that he finds in archives, manifests, and the Atlantic's recorded history—are being employed to restore not just history but a people. This cauterizing of wounds interests Asamoah as he writes:

> In the water, the history of silence was written
> by the first Black family to dissolve in it.
> Hear me: I did not come to sell you sea salt for the price of a country.
>
> If the ship manifest is thirsty, give it seawater.
> We do not pray for the ship manifest to mourn us,
> we only ask for our names back.
> ("In the water the sun cannot hide its bruises")

Asamoah forms a poetic rooted in uncovering the erased history of this encounter between Western colonizing powers and West African cities. For Asamoah, the voices of women are most dominant—women who were resistant to colonialism; who, like his grandmother, were held for their rebellion; and those like Yaa, who died in 1921 in forced exile in the Seychelles at the hands of the British. Here is what the archive yields in poetry: Asamoah creates music that does not dismantle the density of "discoveries" of the past.

Asamoah is writing from the position of a man who, though rooted in Ghana, considers himself relationally (as in Yaanom) a part of the African diaspora when he visits Elmina Castle. "At Elmina Castle I Bled," he reverses the typical trajectory of the New World African who returns to Africa torn between a sense of pilgrimage and the feeling of being a tourist. The speaker at Elmina Castle feels alienated by loss of language. Asamoah, the Ghanaian with his Twi, still encounters the rupture of language—one that is both literal and symbolic: "I put my fingertip against the / markings on every wall here / and beg for translation."

The poems that invoke spaces like Jacksonville, Detroit, and Virginia, must find a way to "translate" the poetry of an African American southern poet like Yusef Komunyakaa, whom Asamoah challenges in "hey Yusef Komunyakaa, *if history is human*, show me her grave." In Komunyakaa's "History is Human," the speaker begins in conversation with a nurse who asks him if he would like a greater dose of painkiller. The poet ponders this question and seems to turn it into an accusation, then expands this encounter, writing:

> And when white America gets hooked,
> our history is human.
> Somewhere a big band strikes up stardust…

Asamoah, now in search of a history that will connect his own in Ghana with the history of African Diaspora in America, wonders where he can find the body of history. It is a petulant question grown out of frustration and lamentation. For him, history, in this instance, is personified as a woman. "Tell me," he demands of Komunyakaa:

> Where she drowned
> Where she isn't a speck in oblivion's vast orgasm
> Where every border is parting of blood
> Where all my poems owe me knives
> Where the blade said: *Look, I slew a beast*—
> waving my mother's country on a pike.

Asamoah's collection interrogates sureties, whether it's questioning the presence of Jesus in Ghana, uncovering the unsettling history of the transatlantic slave trade in archives and monuments, recognizing the complications of modern Ghanaian politics with its coups and revolutions, or, finally, facing the meaning of God in "Prayer is a dagger meant for God's ears," in which he quotes Ghanaian rapper Kwame Ametepee Tsikata in an epigraph. The poem ends thick with questioning:

> And we pray, we soil his white dress with his own blood.
> Wherever we plant our God, a knife germinates.
>
> If God exists, he keeps it to himself behind grief's eyelids,
> if grief blinks, he falls off his perch, but grief's eyes are always sealed shut.
>
> Mother said: In this dust country, smoke from our burning flesh is television
> static in the eyes of a God whose only answer to our prayer is a change of the channel.

One has the sense that Asamoah is a poet who will not be contained by silence. There is ambition in these poems, and a venturesomeness in his willingness to confront matters that offer no easy answers. We have here a poet of great promise.

YAANOM

The last night of their voyage cast shadows
onto *Virginia's* feet. Full moon turned Yaanom to stone gods falling
from my child eyes. Their loose teeth, cemeteries in the spleen of a soft sea.
The sold sails in their blood made song for devil grass
on the footpath to Elmina, Osu, Sekondi-Takoradi, from Anokyekrom
horse calves stretched away from this red circus stolen
from our night's chimpanzee palms. The fog was rock salt. Fog like British frogs.
And in the bluest vein of that night,
I was carrying these poems through a sunset,
to show them what the end of the world looks like.

DZIN

Jesus dismounts his Caucasian horse and walks
over the gulf of Guinea to *Osu, Cape Coast, Elmina* . . .
What kind of mother is a wooden ship?

How many miscarriages before *Jamestown,*
Virginia, Downing Street?
How many false gods did they melt into a whip?

In the *Jesus* name,
we're foot soldiers in the holy dust of Agorkoli's ruin.
Hallelujah! We're lost.

I soak my mouth in the gulf of Guinea and let it bloat my grief.
I spend its language in both sleep & wokeness.
Every sentence I inherit is force-fed.

When I cast a spell with mother,
my tongue returns to me, briefly, a smoke horse.
In my mother's language I have no sugar left to make thrones out of
without capsizing British American ships.

In the *Jesus* name,
the first British slave ship to arrive in Africa was *JESUS of Lübeck,*
chartered by Queen Elizabeth I to slavers in 1562;
they came—literally—in the name of *Jesus!*

TESTIMONY

In my mother's garden, there's a bioluminescent wound in the loam
through which God spies on the world.
I am the door. Trapped like ruined hawk eyes.
She hands me a murder shovel, says: *bury the witness.*
I bury my own feet inside the hole and stick out my tongue
to blend in with the Madagascar periwinkles;
to camouflage myself from God's salacious yet unsweet garden gaze.
Before then, an angel, shrilling, wings dark as vampire bats,
creeps through the wound and begins to steal our flowers;
when the unfolded moonlight fingers the dandelion heads he is gathering,
it looks like a Black woman picking cotton on a plantation,
held at the neck by a memory as hideous as a snake in the garden.

BLESS THE TIDE THAT BLESSES THE BOAT WITH WREATHS

Bless the kiss that betrayed saltwater sailors
Bless the liquid cross we nail our voices to
Bless the furrows in the burning blue flame of Gulf of Guinea
Bless names we left in the dark narrowness

Bless *The Boy Who Spat in Sargrenti's Eye*
Bless the fishes who waited for us to drown
before eating through our eyeballs

Bless the white woman at the landing beach
of the British colony of Virginia, who said,
*Here's some water, but you can't have any
till our God falls in love with your dark skin
and blesses the halo around your neck*

THE END OF THE WORLD LOOKS LIKE SAILS

The shadows crowd on the shore,
pressing their lips against the bosom of the sea.
—*Kwesi Brew*

We're all dust in a dust
country. How much dirt

makes a country a home?
Mother says, *Not this much.*

Our blood is a disappeared mark on a map.
Every day a border shapeshifts somewhere,

some line crossed,
ink becomes towers,

towers become blame,
blame becomes profit,

profit becomes God,
God becomes dust.

The dust is gone,
made off with the ship manifest

with all our names on it.

IN THE WATER THE SUN CANNOT HIDE ITS BRUISES

The Atlantic is a tall trapdoor in my flesh.
I cauterize it with the morose of my chieftains.

The ship manifest reads: 100 negro slaves in total:
66 male negros, 28 female negros, 6 children;
21 bags of rosemary, 200 palettes of rubber.

They lived on the white bark of it.
The Atlantic is a big blue vein,
when punctured right, it prays.

The water keeps the secrets they take from us.
How many rib bones of the oceans have we broken
with wooden ghosts?

In the water, the history of silence was written
by the first Black family to dissolve in it.
Hear me: I did not come to sell you sea salt for the price of a country.

If the ship manifest is thirsty, give it seawater.
We do not pray for the ship manifest to mourn us,
we only ask for our names back.

DOOMSDAY DEVICE
in memoriam Menhyia, February 4–6, 1874. Asante Kotoko, kum apem, a apem bɛ ba.

I imagine Kumase must have kissed silence the way new butterfly bones break after the British hellfire. The city, like the unfinished flesh of something hatched from the moon's skull. I imagine the market tress sirening in their live-coal pelts, branches snapping like the cleaved heads of dead kings gone to Seychelles Island.

Children exploding where they play; what once was their eyes now alcoves filled with wild bats on fire. The stench of the baked crops like a tortured sea. Mothers feeding their newborns their own vomit. Husbands swallowing torches on their wives breasts. The sky sealed shut and roasted red clay. And the birds, the birds are always the first people to lose the sky. Something, skyless, wounded, self-immolation marched from Accra to Cape Coast to Kumase; a flame born seasick and British.

My nanankansowa said: There was rain coming down like paratrooper elephants the night that followed. Darkness bawling its eyes out, thunder and lightning like two mirrors kissing their teeth as they crushed into each other. And the fire did not wash out; could not wash off; *we remember, we remember*. But before then, our ancestors gazed upon Garnet Wolseley and hurled spit at him as if it was a doomsday device.

YAA

(Warrior, mother, intellectual, politician, rebel, farmer, queen. Died in exile from Ghana on October 17, 1921, on an archipelago of Seychelles, off the coast of East Africa).

The goddess breaks her bullet in two,
shares it, like the man-breast flesh of night,
with me.
I take it, protracted, eat it without language
and bleed no dialect into her *Lord* eyes.
The title is salt on the page. I lick it with my lisp.
My God! They kill women they cannot unname.
Yaanom knew the gossip Eden whispered.
Eden said, *Banished bride*; a bullet exiled from heaven.
In Seychelles,
Eve caresses Nana Yaa Asantewaa's hair, turns it into a gun,
and unbraids it in the mouths of *Brits*.
Her bones, moon-dense bullets, sprouting,
when they put her in the ground.

AHWENEPA NKASA

Silence weeps like a distant grenade
and my ears bleed like holes guns make.

My grandmother slingshots spit onto the lips of British colonial guard.
His sharpened shoe makes holes in my grandmother, thus, my mother is born
    with a limp.

In a true story, my grandmother is taken to *America*, not the morgue.
She bleeds while she tells us about revolution.

When grandmother was taken for *disturbing the peace*,
I did not mourn,
I was not born.

DIXCOVE(RY)
Fort Metalen Kruis, 1683

Come split with me this blue metal spleen of *Dixcove*,
approximately 35 kilometers from Sekondi-Takoradi;
one crucifix, two named heads.
Which means, approximately 35 kilometers
from *Fort Orange, Around the Fish,*
close to *Fort Batenstein*, to *Fort George*,
to *Forte de Santo António de Axim*, to *Fort Apollonia* in Beyin,
to *Fort San Sebastian*, to *Fort Nassau, Ahomka Fie*.
15 Dutch Cemetery Rd, Elmina:
Fort Coenraadsburg also *Fort de São Tiago de Mina*:
a Portuguese chapel built in honor of Saint Jago,
situated opposite the *Elmina Castle* to protect her from attack.
Approximately 35 kilometers
to the promontory breasts of an *Ahanta* mermaid.
The impure gold of its teats. Its Anglo-Dutchess.
It is said iron that did not rust became a country;
a country which does not rust becomes a cage.

PRINCE TOWN/POKESU

After John Canoe or John Kenu or Johann Kunny or John Conrad or Johann Cunny or Jean Cunny or January Konny or John Conni, Junkanoo

On 1 January 1681, a *Brandenburger* expedition of two ships arrived in *Pokuse* not far from *Sekondi-Takoradi*, *Gold Coast*, and built *Fort Groot Fredericksborg*—after *Prince Frederick William I*—on the fused throat between *Axim* and *Cape Three Points*. Then came an Ancestor, in 1708, John Canoe or *John Kenu* or *Johann Kunny* or *John Conrad* or *Johann Cunny* or *Jean Cunny* or *January Konny* or *John Conni, Junkanoo*; when a people are terrified by a *truth*, they make many names to warn themselves of it: Ahanta hunter, *Prussia* stone King, a Kraken constricting fleets of European battleships for almost 20 years. Oh mystery merchant of unseeded repose, show me your cannons and I will show you your body.

AT ELMINA CASTLE I BLED

I climb like sea salt
up bedrock bigger than the moon, I swear.
My feet clomp upon the good gray teeth of the old gods:
I want them to hear my coming, my dead.
I lift my eye unto the belly of the titan rocks
and my secret splits the sky.

Every blood-beaten door I walk into clanks
like hyena chuckles, hyenas that once had cannons for throats.
The blood-clean wind comes in crying, its tears—our family heirloom.
How many bad beginnings start with the god who made the Atlantic?

I touch the walls to feel their skin;
it is not a caress, but it is close to its secret.
There is something about the static
in these dark wells and the sound of our blood.
How name lost its meaning and not its music.

This place has a name, those held in it had none.
I put my fingertip against the markings on every wall here
and beg for translation.
I press till I lose feeling in my forefinger—
blood, my only remittance.

Then I hear them,
they call to me: *Bleed with us.*
On the shore I hold out my forefinger
and let my blood fall onto God's tongue.

ALL THE SAINTS OF ELMINA CASTLE ARE WET

All the blood is a black road through the Atlantic.
All the saints are fishes folded in a wave.
All the gods must be sweet cows slaughtered with silence.
All the boats are a startled sword-slice of history.
All the galleons are red lipstick on the ocean floor.
All the caged bird songs are unmarked graveyards.
All its heads are blonde.
All the gunpowder in my prayer is wet with saltwater.
All the saints of Elmina Castle are wet.

YAANOM II

Our kings' bullets invited *Ahmed Suale* to crawl and his blood did.
It climbed my mouth and every drop we drank was his country.
Everywhere a drop stopped is my country.
My womb is the postcolonial banter in the mouths of false gods.
My idols climb out of me, crawling.
I love my country the way silence crawls into a body and gives it borders.
I climb the scattered border of my blood to come see you.
I crawl through you, o blur country, into God's blind spot.
I thought your claws were my birthplace.
So I crawled into your arms, face first, my severed head—your national anthem.

REQUIEM

for Laura Adorkor Kofi of Asofa, Greater Accra, Ghana

    I follow the red convoy in the *Asofa* sun.
Oh my tiny missionary massacre.
Pilgrim through *Asofa,* by way of Ghana, through Detroit,
    through Jacksonville, to dust,
like a bullet
sent from a voice in a bird flame's head.
    Oh matriarch, your forever cage is a tribute to the American sun,
and Jacksonville's Old City Cemetery is its coldest wound
for which this remedy to an American prophecy:
    We hold these truths to be self-evident that all men are created sequels
to an American gun
    that cannot outlive us.

HEY YUSEF KOMUNYAKAA, *IF HISTORY IS HUMAN,* SHOW ME HER GRAVE

        Show me where her blood is shallowest
        Where they split our atoms with new names
        Where she drowned
        Where she isn't a speck in oblivion's vast orgasm
        Where every border is parting of blood
        Where all my poems owe me knives
        Where the blade said: *Look, I slew a beast—*
        waving my mother's country on a pike.

MƐNI AATELE NI ABOOO?
So much there is we must atone.
—Kofi Nyidevu Awoonor

Not because J.J. Rawlings
did it the darkest.

Not because
he is the only mountain with language.

Not because his people spoke:
let the blood flow.

Our flag began with blood
and has remained there, from the beginning.

My mother told me: *I chanted, too, in June of '79:*
If I couldn't have the gold and green, give me the blood then.

Mɛni aatele ni abooo?
What is carried on the head to the market,

is not always for sale?
It may be a crown of thorns for those we crucified.

PRAYER IS A DAGGER MEANT FOR GOD'S EARS
Pastor says fast and prayer—but I want a faster way.
—Kwame Ametepee Tsikata (M.anifest), "Don't Follow Me"

So it begins, my prayer:
Father, please rinse my blood off your rainbow.

In my village the women overthrow God with prayer.
They were the first gods to live as humans; before *Jesus* attempted it.

They eat the empty sirens of our grief.
Their daughters are tantrums clogging the Lord's *Answering Machine*.

We're entitled children of a father whose face is ozone;
prayer is a dagger meant for God's ears.

And we pray, we soil his white dress with his own blood.
Wherever we plant our God, a knife germinates.

If God exists, he keeps it to himself behind grief's eyelids,
if grief blinks, he falls off his perch, but grief's eyes are always sealed shut.

Mother said: In this dust country, smoke from our burning flesh is television
    static
in the eyes of a God whose only answer to our prayer is a change of the channel.

MAGICIAN IN INESCAPABLE SKIN

For you can draw a gun round any town or country
For you can draw a gun which the sun makes hot,
high above the town.
—Kojo Laing

The town glitches, becomes gunpowder.
At the gunplayground they play dumb, we play dead.
It is hard to breathe, but it is harder to believe in God.
Sons: Kofi Awoonor, Ahmed Suale, Eric Ofotsu; pummeled
into a hunting season around my neck.
They are the history of the silver pallor of musket smoke
as angels wash eternal red off their black feathers.
The guns stretched fire into a feast.
The trick is a white chalk encirclement of my foregone tongue.
A candle outlives me by a long life. My wings are unhistoric.
I'm the magician in inescapable skin.
If I cannot escape the red water,
let borla birds take my fragments for nesting
inside the red blood cell of the sun.

Endnote:
Ahmed Suale, a journalist, and Eric Ofotsu, who suffered from mental illness, are two innocent young Ghanaian men who were murdered in 2019 and 2020, respectively. Suale and Ofotsu were killed by gunshots similarly to poet Kofi Awoonor, who was murdered in a terrorist attack by al-Shabaab militants in 2013 at the Westgate shopping mall in Nairobi while he was participating in the Storymoja Hay festival, a celebration of writing and storytelling.

THE TREE

I see the giant tree rising into a sky solid with memory...
He is the storm over the tight mouth widening...
He is the hard, harsh bird, hushed.
—Kojo Laing, "Resurrection 1972"

My tongue is a red banner in the coming wind,
and the motherland is the fire that burns it to keep warm.
My grandmother's hut is sand in my eyes.
The wizards open their mouths and feed me mirrors; all my problems look like me.
Their teeth are capsules filled with ashes.
The little bombs at the corner of my mouth tick without language.
And the priests marry merriment.
We become birds of blood quietness; we citizens of a failing poem.

I landed far from the tree and lost my tongue to the fall.
And the tree called me good fruit.
And the tree leaves are butcher blades.
And the tree performs my dispatch.
And the tree does not talk, does not march.
And its fruits keep rolling away from it.
And the wind that blows the red banner, shakes the tree.
And the tree writhes to the coming whisper.
And all the birds of luxury fall out of the tree.
And the birds are countrymen who have evolved to keep their wings silent.
And they clutch their quietness tightly, lest it falls from them into the dust country
and abolishes the wizards in the tree.

Tonight, revolution is the string at the fingertips of E.T. Mensah.
And if the old world ends in dance, bury me where my country died.

GLOSSARY

Yaanom: a Twi word for folks or ancestors, depending on the context of its usage.

Elmina, Osu, Sekondi-Takoradi, Anokyekrom: names of towns in Ghana.

Dzin: a Mfantse word for "name." Mfantse is a Twi dialect spoken by the indigenous people of the Central Region of Ghana.

Menhyia: the Twi name for the location on which the palace of the Asante king is situated; also the name of the palace.

Nanankansowa: a Twi word for great-grandparent.

Asante Kotoko, kum apem, a apem bɛ ba: Asante Porcupine (warriors), kill a thousand, and a thousand shall come.

Ahwenepa nkasa: good waist beads do not make noise (do not talk).

Mɛni aatele ni abooo?: a question in Ga, the language of the Ga people in Ghana, that directly translates to "what is carried on the head (for hawking) and yet its sale is not called out by its vendor?"

The Boy Who Spat in Sargrenti's Eye: the title of a historical novel by Ghanaian–South African author Manu Herbstein, published in 2014 by Techmate Publishers, Ltd.

ACKNOWLEDGMENTS

An earlier version of "Ahwenepa nkasa" appeared in *Writers Space Africa*.

Earlier versions of "The End of the World Looks Like Sails" and "At Elmina Castle I bled" first appeared in *Lolwe*.

"All the saints of Elmina Castle are wet" first appeared in *20:35 Africa: An Anthology of Contemporary Series*, Vol. VI.